verse noir
david rachels

Verse Noir original edition
　published in 2010.

Verse Noir Expanded Edition
　published August 2017 by
　Automat.Press.

©2017 David Rachels.

Cover design by
　Augustus Rachels.

All rights reserved.
ISBN 978-0-9993209-0-7

Automat Catalog #A013
V5.0
0 9 8 7 6 5 4 3 2

Published by

Automat.Press
//automat.press
Austin, Texas

Monkeys

If you put
One million monkeys
In a room with
One million typewriters
Sooner than you think
The monkeys will use
Those typewriters to
Kill each other.

Setting

The kidney-stoned sky
Squeezed out the rain
One drop at a time
While the wind howled
The pain of the clouds.

Vocabulary

There are words
I have seen
But know not
What they mean:
Pagoda.
Itinerary.
Nuance.
Philatelist.
Penultimate.
Adirondack.
Mercy.

Dad

For my twelfth birthday
My old man gave me
A pair of brass knuckles
That were not really brass
And two issues of Playboy
Missing their centerfolds.

He called it a scholarship.

Hate

If I do not
Hate you
Then you are
Still alive.

Promise

A promise is
A down payment on
A lie.

Experience

People who think
That yelling and screaming
Are the same thing
Have never screamed.

Ambition

At first
My ambition
Was to live
To see thirty.

Later
My ambition
Was to care
Whether
I lived
To see thirty.

Achievement

My lifetime
Achievement award
Is the existence of
My lifetime.

First

The first time you kill
You wonder if
You can actually do it but
Once you have done it then
You wonder why
You never did it before.

Value

She judged value
Not in dollars
But in lives
Not in how much
She would pay
But in how many
She would kill.

Parts

When a woman is all
Adjectives and verbs
The nouns of the thing
Never seem to matter.

Night

The night
Can never be
Darker than
Your soul.

Union

He was left
High and dry.

She was found
Low and wet.

Think

He was not paid to
Think.

He was paid to
Kill.

And if he ever
Caught himself thinking
While he was killing
Then he knew he was doing
Something wrong.

Vision

Everything looks
The same
When your eyes
Are closed.

Locks

Before you lock
Your doors tonight
Consider the pro and the con.

The pro is that your locks
Will keep you safe
For a minute or maybe two.

The con is that I do not like
People who waste my time.

Tears

If I should happen
To make you cry
I know how
To make you stop.

Soulmate

He asked if she would
   marry
A man who killed people
   and
She said only if
She got to watch.

Wedding

Something old
Something new
Something stolen
Someone dead.

Broad

Broad hips
Sink ships.

Yet

No hips
No hope.

Cycle

Whenever I kill a man
I celebrate by
Killing another man
And so on.

Truth

She would never use a
Silencer because silencers
Tell lies.

Her gun told the
Truth loud and ugly and
She refused to
Silence the truth.

Drink

I do not care
If the glass
Is clean.

Love

Love means having
To say you are sorry
Every minute of your life.

Cards

Never deal
A man
Two aces
Of spades.

Cardsharp

He would play
Poker with you
As long as
You did not cheat
Better than him.

Respect

The only way to
Earn his respect was to
Try to kill him but
If you succeeded
In the killing
It was no use to
Have the respect of
A dead man and
If you failed
In the killing
Then the dead man
Would be you.

Command

He spoke
Only
In verbs.

Fists I

He punched
More often
Than he spoke
Because
His fists
Were more
Articulate.

Fists II

The strength of
Your punch
Is a function of
The weakness of
Its recipient.

Purpose

Bones and silence
Were made
To be broken.

Time

If you asked him why
He wore watches on both
   wrists
He would tell you only that
They were synchronized.

Mainline

When you were a kid
You were afraid
Of needles.

Can you believe it?

Policy

She would kill any man if
The price was right but
She would kill a woman
   only if
She was in the mood.

Soul

When he said he would steal until

There was nothing left to steal

She asked who had stolen his soul.

He laughed and said that

No one had stolen his soul though

A frustrated few had tried.

She shook her head and said

They can't steal your soul because

You don't have a soul.

He laughed again and said

They can't steal my soul because

I pawned it in a shop

Over on fifty-ninth street.

Secret

The secret
To keeping a secret
Is keeping it secret
That you know a secret.

Stairs

Whenever the elevator was broken
He was certain that
Someone was trying to kill him.

He would move up the stairs
Slowly and quietly and
Wonder why stairs are forever
Turning back on themselves and
Making corners and shadows where
People can hide.

He would wish that stairs
Could be built up and up
Straight like a ladder where
If someone kills you
At least you see it coming.

Sleep

He thought that
He could learn to
Sleep with one eye
Open.

It turned out that
The challenge was to
Sleep with one eye
Closed.

Friend

A friend is someone who
Currently
Has no plans to kill you.

Outline

When I move
To a new town
The cops run
Out of chalk.

Mistake I

He is lying on the floor
Bleeding out
When our eyes meet
And when I see his look
Is neither anger nor fear
But surprise and confusion
I realize that
I have shot the wrong guy
Again.

Mistake II

When you kill the wrong
    guy
No one cares much if
No one knew him and
Your apology is sincere and
You get it right the second
    time.

Gold

Her breasts were like gold
Soft and heavy and coveted
   and
Redeemable for cash.

Last

The last man he murdered was
Himself.

It was not suicide because
He did not want to die.

What he wanted was to be the
Most heartless killer of them all.

And what could be more heartless than
Killing himself when
He wanted to live?

He said all this in his
Murder note.

Veteran

I quit the army and

Became a hit man because

The pay was better and

There was a better chance that

The people I killed would

Actually deserve it.

Brevity

If you write
Your diary in
Your own blood
Be succinct.

Training

An amateur can kill
With a gun.

A professional can kill
With an unloaded gun.

Foreplay

I like to peel off her
Sheer black stockings
So that I can
Put them on my head.

Nose

If I could smell
Like dogs can smell
Then I would
Hold my breath.

Desire

I will never want
To see you naked
More than I want
You to see me.

Object

If you
Will be
A sex
Object
Then so
Will I.

Size

I am always
Just as big as
I need to be.

Allowance

When he was a kid he kept
   his money in a
Leather pouch and his
   parents gave him
Twenty-five cents every
   week and
He always made them pay
   with
Nickels.

His parents thought that
He was not very bright and
   that
He wanted the nickels
   because
Five nickels seemed like
   more money than one
Quarter.

His parents could never
   have imagined that
Money was not money to
   him but
Weight and

Five nickels weigh more
    than one quarter and

The more his pouch
    weighed the

Heavier it landed on

Heads.

Crowds

She would blend
Into crowds
At first
But stand out
In the end
When she was
The only one
Still standing.

Clap

Some people
Will applaud
Anything.

Eye

His soul was like an eye
Open too long
Tired and out of focus
Shot through with
Streaks of blood.

Corpse

He looked like
Someone had
Killed him
Twice.

Color

She wore lipstick
In several places.

Communication

His eyes said
Live
But his hands said
Die.

Focus

He would have been
A master criminal
If only he had been
Castrated.

Outnumbered

Two breasts
One brain.

Party

I hit him with a baseball
    bat
Like he was a piñata and
His guts were candy.

Discrimination

Not
All blood
Tastes the same.

Criteria

He would sleep with any
   woman who
Had short dark hair and
   who
Had large breasts and who
Was not his mother.

Knowledge I

There are
Things you
Do not
Want to
Know.

Knowledge II

The most
Important lessons
Are learned
By dying.

Knowledge III

Learn slow
Die fast.

Happy

The opposite
Of
Trigger happy
Is
Death happy.

Wisdom

Every day that you live you
Try to remember what you
   did on
The days you didn't die.

Looter

He moved to San Francisco
And found a job
As a short order cook
To make ends meet
While he waited
For an earthquake.

Mercury

She moved like mercury
On a china plate
Poisonous and
Easy to break.

Men

She wanted to
Like men
But
She never
Had the chance.

Bricks

The first thing he did
After he bought the big house
Was to brick up the windows.

Neighbors thought that
He did not want them to see in
But the truth was
He did not want to see out.

Honeymoon I

On his wedding night
He beat his bride just to
Get it out of the way.

Honeymoon II

On her wedding night
She beat her groom just to
Get it out of the way.

Mild

Divorce
Is the
Mildest
Solution.

Bird

He got a parrot but
It never talked.

We asked
How come
It never talks?

He said
Because the bird
Knows better.

Gun

My dream is to have a gun
Made of flesh and bone.

Holding it will be like
Holding a man's hand.

When I squeeze the handle
It will be warm.

And when I pull the trigger
It might pull back.

Brass

Brass?
Not brass.
His balls
Were made
Of lead.

Vow

When he promised
Always to protect me
I had no idea
He would take it
So seriously.

Beautiful

Blood can be beautiful until
You know what it is unless
Knowing what it is makes it
Even more beautiful.

Smarts

I had no idea
How much brains
He had
Until
I saw them.

Ego

If you kill
A man's ego
You had better
Finish the job.

Salvation

When he said he was a
   preacher
I called him my brother and
   told him that
I too am in the business of
Heaven and hell.

When he asked my
   denomination
I told him that
Women are my heaven and
Guns are my hell though
Sometimes these roles can
Mysteriously reverse.

Trees

I am a city boy.

If money grew on trees
I would still hate trees
Though I would not mind
Raking leaves.

Soap

She was a country girl but

She used words

Filthy words

Enough to send her mother

Running to the general store until

It ran out of soap.

Of course I knew these words

Having heard them many times but

Always from city men and

Never in these combinations.

City

A city is forever
In the process
Of becoming
A cemetery.

Chicago

He says he is from Chicago
   as if
He expects me to be
   impressed or
Maybe even scared.

I shake my head and laugh
   and
Spit near his shoes and say
You think people die only in
   Chicago?

Sky

The sky
Is only
Another
Ceiling.

Gifts

When someone
Gives you a gun
Other gifts become
Unnecessary.

Car

A woman is like a car.

If she gets you
Where you need to go
You have no right
To complain.

Brain

Whenever he ate
A peanut butter sandwich
He thought about death
Because everything made him
Think about death.

Specialty

His specialty was
Kicking.

He carried a gun
Only to make
People lie down
So that he
Could kick them
To death.

Then he would
Shine his shoes.

Keys

I have three keys.

The first opens my house.

The second opens my car.

The third opens everything else.

Motion

His love moved
In and out
Like the tides
Steady but
Too slow.

Bachelor

He would have
Married a gun
But he could
Never find one
With a big
Enough barrel.

Resolution

When I got
My sentence
The first thing
I did was
Quit smoking
Because I
Have got to
Stay alive
Long enough
To kill the
Bastard who
Put me here.

Numbers

He told us that in his other
   life

He had been an actuary
   and

Once he explained what
   that meant

He announced he was
   developing a formula to

Tell us our life expectancies
   based on

All kinds of numbers
   including

How many bets we took and

How much those bets were
   for and

How many drugs we sold
   and

How much those drugs
   weighed and

How many men we had
   killed so

We filled out every last
   survey.

We should have known that

He was a cop.

Request

For his last meal
He requested
The warden's wife.

Multiplication

Having kids
Just means
More people
To kill.

Hurry

If you
Let them
Live too
Long they
Kill you.

Tally

He had tally marks tattooed
On both of his arms
One arm with marks for
Each man killed
The other with marks for
Each woman conquered
But he could never keep track of
Which arm was which.

Straight

She had her head on
Straight
Because her husband
Found her a good
Psychiatrist.

He had his head on
Straight
Because his wife
Found him a good
Mortician.

Search

They dragged
The lake
But all
They found
Was hate.

Kindness

When I tried
To kill a man
With kindness
He shot me.

Philosophy

I enjoy doing
What I am doing
Even more than you
Want me to stop.

Circle

People kill people
Because
People are people.

Emotion

Hate
Buys the gun.

Love
Pulls the trigger.

Holes

He could
Make them
And
He could
Fill them.

Mantra

Corpses
Cannot
Kill.

Mouth

The best thing
About her
Was her mouth.

Lips
Full and ruby red
Teeth
White and straight
Tongue
Soft and skilled.

Men took
One look at her
And knew she gave
Good alibi.

Cost

Life is cheap because
Bullets are.

Talent

She got the job
Even though
She could dance.

Skill

When I got into
This line of work
I had no idea
How much time
I would spend
Shoveling.

Distinction

Innocence is killing
For profit.

Guilt is killing
For pleasure.

Smart

Smart is
Less important than
Not stupid.

Whistle

I wish that I could
Whistle while I work
But then you would
Hear me coming.

TGIF

There is no
Good day
To die.

There is no
Bad day
To kill.

Difference

The difference
Between cop
And criminal
Is salary.

Bravery

Better to be alive
Than brave.

Zero

Nihilism is
A function of
Age and
Bank balance.

Thief

When they put pennies
On his dead eyes
The pennies disappeared
Even though there was
No one in the room.

Honor

There is honor
Among thieves
Who want
To live.

Guests

Thieves make the best
Dinner guests
Because the best
Dinner guests
Know when to leave.

Pause

Stop look and listen
Before you

Pain I

Sometimes
The only thing
Worse than dying
Is not dying.

Pain II

Does it hurt more
To get shot
In the belly
Or the kneecap?

Yes.

Pain III

Pain is
The way
Your body says
Shoot me
Again.

Church

Whenever he saw a church
He would cross the street
To avoid it.

He was afraid that
He would go inside
But he could never say
Whether he was
Afraid for himself or
Afraid for the church.

Crossbreed

She was
Part woman
And
Part human.

Travel

It is good to know
How to run
But it is better to know
How to choose a direction.

Limitation

He had the speed
To outrun bullets
But not the stamina.

Knife

I laughed when he pulled
His Swiss Army knife
So he showed me
What a man can do
With a miniature corkscrew
And a pair of tiny scissors.

Priority

My suit will never
Cost more than my gun.

Art

Of all the things I steal

I most enjoy stealing art

Because anyone who owns art

Deserves to have it stolen.

Horizontal

In bed
She was
Good but
Dishonest.

Sale

His life was one long
Fire sale of the soul.

Every smoke-damaged
   moral
Every water-logged scruple
Was priced to sell.

Sales

Profit margin
Is highest on
Things you
Do not own.

Home

Home is the place where
They always look first.

Talk

Bullets never
Negotiate.

Objectivity

If I were
Objective
I would kill
Everyone.

Math

The answers to
My word problems
Are always expressed
In whole numbers.

Sometimes

Sometimes
People need
Killing.

Sometimes
You need
Practice.

Lies I

When I saw that
She would believe
Anything I said
I outdid myself with lies
Each more extravagant and
More absurd than
The one before.

When I realized that
Her belief was a lie
I began telling the truth and
When I was certain that
Her belief was still insincere
I knew that
I had won.

Lies II

He was determined to tell
Every lie he knew.

Anything that remained
Would be the truth.

Hell

To an optimist hell
Is an idea.

To a pessimist hell
Is a place.

To a realist hell
Is a goal.

Job

I live my life
Resigned to the fact that
Prison is my job and
Parole is a vacation that
Always seems to end
Too soon.

God

When he saw God
He pulled his revolver and
Took a shot even though
God can dodge bullets.

He knew that he was
Wasting his time but
He thought that maybe
God would give him
Credit for trying.

Safety

You cannot protect it
If you show it
To every woman who asks.

Nature

You want to hear
A nature poem?
Try this:
My nature is to
Fuck you up and
Steal your shit.
There's your
Nature poem.

Rules

I

If crime does not pay
Then you have chosen
The wrong crime.

II

Prefer adding
To subtracting.

III

Prefer multiplying
To dividing.

IV

Whenever possible
Do your own math.

V

Try it
Before you
Steal it.

VI

Function
Over form.

VII

Form over
Personality.

VIII

Never teach an old dog
New tricks.

IX

Never teach a young dog
Tricks.

X

Trust nothing that
Curves.

XI

Deny even
Your denials.

XII

Never forget that
Your retirement plan
Is death.

www.ingramcontent.com/pod-product-compliance
Lightning Source LLC
Chambersburg PA
CBHW050538300426
44113CB00012B/2171